The Face
Of Seven

Monique S. Bailey

ISBN: 978-1-953181-07-7

DEDICATION

This book is lovingly dedicated to my immediate family. *To my husband*: thank you for being by my side every step of the way. Your love for me is undeniable, and I thank God every day for creating you just for me. I don't know how I could have made it without you.

To my eldest, Monea': you have been more than a daughter. You have been a shoulder to lean on, and at times, you've taken on the role as a mother to comfort me. Your feedback and input on writing this book will always be appreciated.

To my baby girl, Desiree: there is a lot that you don't quite understand just yet, but you've done your best to show me that you are willing to listen and follow my requests. You have allowed me to give you numerous hugs and kisses, even when I get on your nerves. I believe that you know that deep down inside I need them, so thank you!

Thank you all from the bottom of my heart.

TABLE OF CONTENTS

INTRODUCTION

The purpose of telling my truth in my first book, *In My Despair*, was to expose the very thing that held me captive for so many years. I grew older in age, but I was still a child in my own thoughts.

If you were ever cut on your leg, arm, or hand, you had to expose that cut to air to heal. Keeping your wound covered would not allow you to heal in the way you needed to. You must first take the band aid off and expose traumatic/problematic moments in your life for your healing to begin.

What I did not know was that the healing process could hurt just as much or even more than the thing that cut me in the first place. Seven rapes, seven different abusers, but only one face was a constant reminder of it all. At first, I could not seem to understand why my last abuser was the one that hurt me the most. Because our shared "circle" was our family, I was constantly reminded of what had been done and the things I hadn't fully let go of. When whatever or whoever hurt you still has access, you may find that your process towards healing won't go as you planned.

I can recall the day I found out my book, *In My Despair*, had been released and was ready to be distributed to the public. I was so thrilled and nervous at the same time. I felt excited because it had taken me over eleven years to finish writing my story. Finally finding the courage to write and share my story made me relive some of the most terrifying times in my life. I would sometimes find myself in a state of gloom, and I eventually started projecting my hurt onto others. There were times when I displaced my anger and lashed out at others who were innocent.

Just as I was, many of you may find yourself fearful of how the world will view you after sharing all that you have been through. After hiding the aspects of myself that were unpleasant, a part of me became frightened at what releasing it all meant. I was a grown woman trying to nurture my inner child that was still bleeding inside.

THE AFTERMATH

Almost immediately after the release of my book, some of my family members expressed their disappointment. In their eyes, I exposed the "family business," which I found odd since it was my life I was talking about. I was scared but no longer ashamed of my story because we all have been through something. My story may not be unique, and by my past circumstances, anyone could have predicted my future. The difference between others and myself is that I serve a God who has kept me. Many nights I have contemplated suicide and homicide, but God saved me from myself, and He has continuously kept me.

Honestly, I had no idea that the aftermath would be so devastating. Based on some responses I received, some made me feel like I was psychotic for doing what I had done. Hearing the words, "*You're not the only one who has ever been raped*" from someone so close hurt me deeply. That statement was true, but it felt insensitive to say while I was pouring out my heart to them. I was offered the opportunity to talk with a psychiatrist at no cost to me, but all I really wanted was to receive a call just to check and see how I was doing, to see if I wanted company or even needed prayer. The lack of empathy was simply unimaginable; I just wanted that one person to say, "*I'm here for you and I love you.*"

I sat and often wondered if the people I love really knew just how much their behavior had stabbed me. I had more people against me than I had on my side, but thank God for those in my household who were my biggest supporters. I eventually spoke with several counselors to help me cope with all that transpired. In counseling, I shared I was told that I shouldn't be acting how I was since I was a pastor now. I didn't understand why my title was a reason for me not to receive the healing that I needed. For me, it was the very reason I needed to be healed from my hurt. I felt that for me to tell others how to begin their healing, I first needed to begin my own.

I realized I had to stop lending my ear to the voices of others and that it was time for me to block out their words so that I could hear the voice of God.

Amazingly, my oldest daughter, Monea', expressed how proud she was of me for having the courage to follow through with my healing process. Her response made me say, "It is what it is." I claimed my hurt and pain because that's who I am!

→ *I am who I am because of it!* ←

Thank you, Jesus! My past did not destroy my future. Even though it hindered my growth for many years, it did not keep me bound.

Early one morning, I heard the voice of God speak to me. He said, "Wake up and start writing."

I pleaded with God, saying, "Lord, I am too tired. I'll do it a little later."

Again, God spoke saying the same thing, so I sat up and rubbed the crust out of my eyes, I lifted my arms to stretch, and as I yawned, God revealed to me that the process to healing for me consisted of nine key points in which I call the C.E.W. Process:

Confession	**E**xpose	**W**ait
Communicate	**E**liminate	**W**illpower
Commitment	**E**xamine	**W**alk in your healing

This C.E.W. process has worked for me, and when a negative thought or feeling appears, I revert to C.E.W. as my cue. I hope that when anyone reflects on the C.E.W. process, they will get their cue to continue on their path of healing. It is so easy to return to the pool of pity where you feel sorry for yourself, anguished, and perhaps bitter. We all have triggers, but how we react to them makes all the difference in the world. Prayerfully by going through these nine steps, you will discover self-awareness and find forgiveness, joy and peace.

You deserve to be completely healed, so take a C.E.W. and go with me through my journey of healing. Perhaps you can find healing for yourself as well.

BEFORE YOU START

"I didn't always fight wisely. My emotions often got the best of me, and I caused damage to others. It was a tough lesson to learn about my heart. Don't try to fight without healing because you'll fight from the wrong position. It doesn't mean you don't need to fight—it just means don't jump in without training."

~Dr. Nina Knight

I pray that as you go through this journey of healing that you have an open heart and an open mind. Cast out all doubt that you can't be healed, because I'm a living witness that you can be!

Take a deep breath. You may have to bring some ugly and hurtful things to the surface, but don't worry, you will bury them.

STEP 1: CONFESSION

A **confession** is when you publicly tell people something that you believe or feel.

James 5:16

"Confess your faults one to another, and pray one for another, that ye may be healed. The effectual fervent prayer of a righteous man availeth much."

It is my belief that confessing is the beginning of your liberation. As the scripture states, the purpose of a confession is that you may be healed. Being healed is not something that can happen overnight, but if you confess and fervently pray, *you will be healed*!

The day I decided to confess, I was in my bedroom, and the door was closed so I could prepare myself to study the word of God. To avoid climbing up and down my high-rise bed, I grabbed everything I needed to read. I sat on my bed, surrounded with study bibles and notebooks spread out everywhere. I closed my eyes and began praying: "*Lord, here I am once again coming before your throne asking that you open up my understanding of your word. Amen!*" I opened the Bible app on my iPad and immediately saw the daily scripture and Tom Elliff's four-day devotional, "Hurting to Healing." I read the sample and thought to myself, "I'll revisit the devotion at a later time." I tried to focus on hearing a word from God, but the more I tried, the more I saw the face of the seven.

I began praying again, asking the Lord to help me focus. Without warning, tears flowed from my eyes. I was telling myself to stop crying. Again, I pleaded, "Lord help me!" I became frustrated because no matter how desperate I was to get out of that negative place in my head, I just couldn't. I felt hopeless and ashamed that I was being held captive by this one person.

I was so angry with myself for losing sight of what

I had sought out to do, which was study! I told God that He had chosen the wrong person to pastor other people. There was no way I could minister to others when I needed to be ministered to. I thought, *How could I encourage others when I needed encouragement, and how could I be strong for others when I wasn't strong for myself? God, you've made a mistake. I'm not ready to walk in this calling.*

God said to me in a soft but firm voice, "I make no mistakes!"

"Okay Lord, then maybe I jumped the gun, and it just wasn't my time to pastor."

Again, God spoke, saying, "Your time is not my time. I make no mistakes!"

I lifted my bowed head and said, "Lord, I've been praying for years to be free of this pain, but I can't break away from it, so God show me how."

My shaken spirit became calm as I took a few deep breaths. I leaned off my bed so that I could reach my nightstand to grab a box of tissues. I cleaned my face, wiping my puffy eyes and blowing my stuffy nose.

Again, taking deep breaths, I said, "Lord, I've listened to others, but now I need to hear from you."

Often, you pray and ask God to do certain things in

your life, but you really don't stop to listen to His instructions. Mainly because you are too busy listening to what others have to say about your situation. When you want to stop the hurt, want your frustration to cease, and want the nightmares to end, you must figure out solutions, even after you've prayed. ***Your biggest mistake is being so eager to heal that you miss what God is telling you.***

In that moment, I repented to the Lord for being disobedient. About 21 or 22 years ago, God told me to confess, and honestly, I didn't because I was offended. I didn't believe that I had anything to confess; I felt I wasn't the one who sinned, therefore I never confessed anything. Almost immediately, the phrase "Confession is good for the soul" came to mind. This phrase is a proverb that advises one to admit their sins honestly because it is therapeutic and will make them feel better.

I asked God to show me what I needed to confess, and He did. My tears of sadness turned into tears of gratitude when He brought to the forefront of my mind that I needed to first forgive myself. What happened to me was not my fault, and I was not to blame. I had to stop lying to myself and to everyone

13

else because I was pretending like the abuse had no effect on me. Even though people knew something happened to me, they had no clue how much pain I was in, and I was suffering because of it. I became a master of smiling in public while suffering in private, but no more! I spoke over my life and proclaimed my deliverance because what I confessed was going to open doors to my future freedom.

Proverbs 18:21

"Death and life are in the power of the tongue:"

Be mindful of the words that come out of your mouth because you have the power to speak life and death into your situation. Public Enemy was on to something when they said, "Fight the Power!" You have to fight. Fight to bring life back into your life—just existing is not enough.

Did you know the enemy cannot read your mind? No, he can't! Therefore, he can only operate with what you say.

If you say you won't succeed, consequently, you won't. If you say you're a failure, then you will fail. If you say no one understands me, then you will attract people that won't understand you.

Negative speaking breeds negativity, while positive speaking will call forth positivity.

Choose to speak positive words, such as:

"I will make it through this."

"With God's help, I know I will smile again."

"The sun will shine again."

"Victory belongs to me."

What do you need to confess to begin your healing process? Be open and honest. Otherwise, you will cheat yourself of the healing you deserve.

Your thoughts:

_____

_____

_____

_____

_____

_____

_____

_____

Prayer: *Lord, I confess that I have not only lied to others, but I've been lying to myself, and I ask that you forgive me. From this day forward, help me to speak the truth. Help me not to hold on to the things of yesterday, but the things of the future. Amen.*

Psalms 119:26

"I have declared my ways, and thou heardest me: teach me thy statutes."

Confession is not for you to just tell God what's going on in your life, because He already knows. He wants you to want the healing that He is offering. Once you tell God what's going on in your life, ask God to give you a teachable heart, and He will hear you.

Psalms 119:29

"Remove from me the way of lying: and grant me thy law graciously."

God can remove deceitfulness from you so that you are no longer under the influence of its power. When you are ready to let all untruth go, God will grant you the grace to operate in truth.

Psalms 32:3-5

"When I kept silence, my bones waxed old through my roaring all the day long. For day and night thy hand was heavy upon me: my moisture is turned into the drought of summer. Selah. I acknowledged my sin unto thee, and mine iniquity have I not hid. I said, I will confess my transgressions unto the Lord; and thou forgavest the iniquity of my sin. Selah."

When you keep silent, your body will feel like it's decaying because of the thoughts you continue to hold on to. The very thing that you are holding onto will play over and over in your head like a broken record. You will find the things that should bring you joy no longer do, and little by little you will dry up and wither away.

Remember: You've asked the Lord to help you stop lying to yourself, and you did so because you cannot begin your journey of healing until you do.

Notes:

_____

_____

_____

_____

_____

_____

_____

_____

_____

_____

_____

_____

_____

_____

_____

_____

_____

_____

_____

_____

_____

_____

_____

STEP 2: EXPOSE

To **expose** something hidden means you uncover it so that it can be seen.

Luke 8:17

"For nothing is secret, that shall not be made manifest; neither any thing hid, that shall not be known and come abroad."

The enemy often held me captive with the secret that I kept hidden from the world, playing with my mind like a little child chasing an imaginary ball. I kept going in circles with my emotions because I knew that exposing the face of seven could destroy a home. It could potentially destroy the relationship between a father and a child, between a husband and a wife, and our family could hate or disown me for airing my dirty laundry.

There were many nights I contemplated taking my own life to protect others. My heart was bleeding like a river, and I was drowning in my own blood. I was trapped between a revolving door, and the only way for me to get out was to push someone else out of my way.

I sat in my room wrapped in a blanket, trying to convince myself that writing my book was the best way to expose what I had been holding on to. The face of seven could no longer rule over my life. The negative comments filled my head like air fills a balloon, and I felt like I was going to explode, so I screamed.

Both of my daughters came running to me.

"Mommy, what's wrong? Are you okay?" they asked.

"Yes, I'm fine," I replied. Desireé, my youngest, walked away like, "Ok, mommy is going through again."

Monea' knew that I wasn't fine, so she sat next to me and said, "Mom, it's going to be okay!" I looked up at her with my bloodshot eyes and shook my head. She said to me, "Mom, sometimes you have to be selfish!" This child was born with a six sense; she knew exactly what I was thinking.

She was right. All these years, I worried about how my truth would hurt others. Meanwhile, my home was slowly being destroyed and my relationship with my husband and my children was tainted. I'm sure there were plenty of days that my husband didn't understand my mood. I wouldn't open up to him completely, so it was hard for him to comprehend how I was feeling. I'm sure if I asked him, he'd say he wanted to call it quits and walk out on me but thank God he didn't. I would often snap at my children without cause. Someone once said, "If you never heal from what hurt you, you'll bleed on people who didn't cut you." I was doing just that.

I was broken into a million pieces, and all I longed for was to be made whole. I didn't even know if that was possible, but I was willing to try.

I can recall being in church on a Sunday morning sitting in the pew while listening to the preacher say, "God sees and knows all! The eyes of the Lord are in every place beholding the evil and the good, and every hidden thing will be uncovered!" Since I believed every word that was said, I would clap with such expectation.

I often wondered how long it would take for God to uncover my hidden secrets. Here's the thing... I think that when the preacher preached that message, they were referring to the hidden sins of the congregation that they wanted to know about, or perhaps it was a scare tactic to get people to confess. In my case, I was hopeful; I eventually noticed that once something was exposed and made the church "look bad," it would always be swept under the rug.

I've learned that when people say things like, *"Turn it over to the Lord and leave it there... God casted it into the sea of forgetfulness... It's under the blood... Forgetting those things which are behind and reaching forth unto those things which are before..."* they are often using tools to keep you silent and powerless. They don't tell you to keep quiet to protect you, but to protect themselves.

Psalms 34:18

"The Lord is nigh unto them that are of a broken heart; and saveth such as be of a contrite spirit."

The Lord is not as far away from you as you may feel that He is. He is always near, even when you may feel that He's not.

Exposure is one of the hardest yet rewarding steps you can take. While confession is unto the Lord, the exposure is unto people. It allows you to breathe again and reclaim your life. Just be sure that you are not exposing someone or something just to be vindictive or malicious. Your healing will lie stagnant because you are doing it for the wrong reasons. However, if you are exposing whatever it is and it's for the benefit of being healed, then great! You decide that your freedom is far more precious than anything that you've been holding on to. Do not worry about what others will think of you, because it will hold you back from receiving the healing you need. You cannot allow the thoughts of others to keep you silent. Speak up! Scream loud, even if no one is listening. God is!

Take a moment and consider who or what you need to expose in your life.

Your thoughts:

_____

_____

_____

_____

_____

_____

_____

_____

_____

_____

_____

_____

_____

_____

_____

_____

_____

_____

_____

_____

_____

_____

Prayer: *Lord, As I lift the lid up off my life to expose what's been holding me captive, I pray I will not be affected by what others think or say and I will continue to trust you in the process as you send a release to my life. Amen.*

Matthew 10:26

"Fear them not therefore: for there is nothing covered, that shall not be revealed; and hid, that shall not be known."

There may be times when you feel a level of fear, believing that what you need to uncover might cause others to dislike or even hate you, but you know that every hidden thing will be exposed.

Ephesians 5:11-12

"And have no fellowship with the unfruitful works of darkness, but rather reprove them. For it is a shame even to speak of those things which are done of them in secret."

Paul is instructing us to not only avoid evil pleasures but rebuke and expose them because our silence is interpreted as approval.

Remember: You're not doing this to be vengeful; you're doing this for your freedom and deliverance.

Notes:

_____

_____

_____

_____

_____

_____

_____

_____

_____

_____

_____

_____

_____

_____

_____

_____

_____

STEP 3: WAIT

To **wait** means that you remain where you are with hope and expectation. So, when God tells us to **wait**, He is asking us to be patient; to have hope and expectation of what He is going to do in and through our lives.

For me, waiting was like walking on a lake bare foot onto a bed of ice in 10-degree weather. Waiting for the ice to melt was uncomfortable and something that made no sense to me. Waiting was something that I didn't want to do because I thought it was impossible.

Lamentations 3:25

"The Lord is good unto them that wait for him, to

the soul that seeketh him."

Juanita Bynum sings a song "I Don't Mind Waiting." When I first heard it, I fell in love with the song even though the lyrics did not ring entirely true within me. I was waiting for *my* change to come. I never wanted to be held captive by my hurt and tormented by the lies, but I was. Each moment that went by that I wasn't free was another moment too long. Unfortunately, those moments turned into hours and the hours turned into days. The days became weeks, weeks became months, and the months turned into years; years of dying slowly, years that I can never retrieve. I was tired of waiting for someone to recuse me, tired of looking at the face of seven nearly every week and tired of waiting for justice to be served. All I wanted was to be free from pretending. It was exhausting to smile and laugh while I was screaming like a person trying to be released from the pits of hell on the inside.

Psalms 37:34

"Wait on the Lord, and keep his way, and he shall

exalt thee to inherit the land: when the wicked are cut off, thou shalt see it."

When we decide to wait on the Lord, we are deciding to trust Him completely, and while we are trusting Him, we should continue to do what pleases Him. If we do this, we will possess the land. When we do all of that, God will vindicate us, and we will see it.

Proverbs 20:22

"I will recompense evil; but wait on the Lord, and he shall save thee."

Waiting is not necessarily hard. We wait all the time; we wait for our food, we wait on a plane, we wait a length of time to see the doctor, we wait on people and a million other things, but when it comes to us waiting for God, it becomes challenging. It forces you to sit with your hands tied. The biggest thing about waiting that I've learned is that God wears a totally different watch than we do. His time is not our time.

I thought I had waited more than enough time for God to step in and change my situation; but there were a few things that I didn't realize:

- *I was "waiting" wrong*; I was having temper tantrums.

- *I was "waiting" my way*; I tried to fix the problem that I had myself. Therefore, I relinquished God from fully being in control.

- *I was not "waiting" patiently*; being impatient had everything to do with my deliverance being delayed.

One day, I was in Staples with my two daughters, and my youngest daughter wanted candy. I told her she couldn't have the candy yet and she had to wait. Well, homegirl flipped completely out in the store causing a scene (temper tantrum). She grabbed the candy off the shelf (tried to fix the problem), and needless to say, she didn't get the candy, but take note. I never told her no. I just told her she had to wait and because of her impatience, she missed out on what she could have had.

Don't flip out because God told you to wait, and in haste, you try to solve the problem on your own, creating a bigger mess. Don't let your impatience keep you from getting what God has for you.

It wasn't until I learned how to wait on God that my situation looked and felt different. Waiting on the Lord will strengthen and develop you. Without Him, we are helpless and hopeless.

Romans 5:3-4

"And not only so, but we glory in tribulations also: knowing that tribulation worketh patience; And patience, experience; and experience, hope:"

While you are waiting on God, wait patiently. Remove yourself from the equation (if you had the power to heal yourself, you'd already be healed) and God will change you while you wait. Answer these three questions, yes/no:

- Are you waiting wrong? _____
- Are you waiting your way? _____
- Are you waiting impatiently? _____

If you answered "no" to any of the questions, then you do not have a problem in that area. If you answered "yes" to any of the questions, then that is the area in which you need to ask God to show you how to wait. Write a prayer for patience.

Your thoughts:

_____

_____

_____

_____

_____

_____

_____

_____

_____

_____

_____

_____ *Amen.*

Prayer: *Lord, I ask that you hear the words that are written and move accordingly. Amen.*

Psalms 27:14

"Wait on the Lord: be of good courage, and he shall strengthen thine heart: wait, I say, on the Lord."

Be patient, be brave and He will strengthen you. Just in case you need to hear it again, **wait**!

Waiting is a muscle; It doesn't work until you exercise it!

Here are a few quotes I'd like to share with you:

"Trust in God's timing. It's better to wait awhile and have things fall into place than to rush and have them fall apart."
~Adam Cappa

"Waiting on God requires the willingness to bear uncertainty, to carry within oneself the unanswered question, lifting the heart to God about it whenever it intrudes upon one's thoughts." ~ Elisabeth Elliot

"The only thing harder than waiting on God is wishing that you did." ~Steven Furtick

Remember: How patient you are while you wait will make all the difference in the outcome. Here's an example of waiting impatiently. Imagine baking a cake and the directions say to bake it at 350 degrees for 30 minutes, but you take the cake out in 23 minutes. You say to yourself oh it's ready because it smells and looks good. However, the cake is not finished baking and you can't eat it because it needed to continue baking for the other 7 minutes.

Be sure not to move ahead of God because you feel good, because you may not be ready to face the next stage in your life.

Notes:

_____

_____

_____

_____

_____

_____

_____

_____

_____

_____

_____

_____

_____

_____

_____

STEP 4: COMMUNICATE

Communication is when you share information with others. **Communicating** involves a sender, a message, and a recipient. This may sound simple, but **communication** is a very complex subject.

Ephesians 4:29

"Let no corrupt communication proceed out of your mouth, but that which is good to the use of edifying, that it may minister grace unto the hearers."

Don't be dishonest or manipulate a situation to benefit yourself. Not only can you bring harm to someone who does not deserve it, but it will also make people not want to trust you.

Once you have made your confession and exposed what you've been holding on to, you can move on to communication. When you communicate with someone, you decide to share information with them. You can be verbal, but there are other ways to communicate. You can use signs, art, writing and even your behavior.

This step may be a little frustrating at first and that's only because you must discover which form of communication will work best for you. Don't get discouraged if someone does not understand or pay attention to what you are trying to relay. Everyone won't interpret the matters of your heart as you expect them to, so you must keep exploring what will work best for you.

Starting at age seven, I encountered some unbelievable things, and when I was nine years old, things took a turn for the worst. How could I possibly explain my first traumatic experience to anyone? I was so afraid to tell what happened to me and for days I kept silent. I went into a mute state where I couldn't talk even though I wanted to. It was as if my mouth had been sewn shut. My mother knew that based on my behavior that something was not right with me, but it wasn't enough to prompt her to ask me detailed questions. So, the only thing that came to me was for me to draw a picture of what happened. I did my best to be as detailed as I could using vivid colors to express what I needed to say.

When my mother saw the drawing, she immediately asked, "Who did this?"

I used two forms of communication, but only one got the attention I desired.

Growing up, there were so many times that I used my behavior to communicate, and most of the time people thought I just wanted attention. I wanted those close to me to see my actions as a cry out for help. Often, I was seen as mischievous. There was a brief time that I used silence to communicate that something was wrong, but it didn't work well on my end because being mute was hard for me to do. I still could not talk about all that had happened to me.

As mentioned earlier, I wrote my story on paper, and it wasn't until after the release of my book that I found my voice. Having my life's story written in black and white was how I communicated everything bottled up inside.

Once you find your voice in whatever form works best for you, it can become tricky because you must discern who you can talk to. Every friend is not a friend, and every family member is not family. You may talk to someone that seems to hear you and understand you, but the moment you turn your back, they're spreading your conversation around to others– not so you can receive additional support, but to have something to gossip about. Many times, the ones you trust play double agent to make you feel they are with you, but everything you say is taken out of context or taken back to the wrong people.

It was hard to get my family to see my pain when other family members were involved because they saw my pain as a problem that can destroy things. They heard what I had to say, but they weren't really listening.

"Any problem, big or small, within a family, always seems to start with bad communication. Someone isn't listening." ~
Emma Thompson

What I have realized about people and their lack of empathy is that it's not always about what you communicate–but about how they feel about what you've told them.

"Effective communication is 20% what you know and 80% how you feel about what you know." ~ Jim Rohn

Proverbs 18:2

"A fool hath no delight in understanding,"

There will be some people that have no interest in understanding what you've been through or are going through, and you must be ok with that and know that they are not the right person to communicate with regarding your problems.

If someone you have spoken with is spoon feeding you negativity, downplaying, or disregarding your story, that maybe a sure sign to leave them alone. Remember, there are two types of people in this world: ones that will pour into you, and ones that will zap you of all your energy, self-respect, and self-worth.

Good communication matters because you'll find that you cannot make the journey alone. It takes a level of boldness to admit that you need help from someone, so be clear on what you need and expect from them. Good communication skills can help resolve the problem or perhaps prevent them from developing.

Prayer: *Lord, show me the best way to communicate with others. Season my words and/or actions with your grace. Amen.*

Write about how you plan to communicate with others:

_____

_____

_____

_____

_____

_____

_____

_____

_____

_____

List three people you *should* communicate with.

1. _____

2. _____

3. _____

List three people you ***should not*** communicate with.

1. _____

2. _____

3. _____

Remember: There are several ways to communicate, so if the first form doesn't work for you, try another form. You deserve to tell your story and speak your peace.

Notes:

_____

_____

_____

_____

_____

_____

_____

_____

STEP 5: ELIMINATE

When you **eliminate** something, you are choosing to get rid of it.

Tara Mackey says that the first step of eliminating something or someone toxic is actually recognizing the fact that it's harming you: "*Toxic people are manipulative and often selfish. They have a hard time owning their feelings or apologizing.*"

If a relationship is weighing on you constantly or bringing you down significantly more than it's building you up, it's time to let go. "*Toxic people are a distraction from your true purpose,*" says Mackey.

I couldn't agree more. When you realize that what you are doing or who you are around is not good for you, you need to make some necessary changes. That means you may have to remove yourself from certain situations.

When I decided to eliminate the face of seven, I didn't do it on a whim. I thought long and hard about what it could do to other relationships that I had. I did not know that some people that I loved all my life would make me feel like an unwanted orphan.

I had to eliminate being around the face of seven because he was toxic for me. I never knew when he would say or do something that would trigger my emotions. It was like I was playing Russian roulette, and once the bullet left the chamber, it would hit my emotions hard, causing me to have sweats, nightmares, and even suicidal thoughts. Many times, I would put a Band-Aid on my bullet wound, which did absolutely nothing because the wound was still there, and it still hurt.

When you choose to eliminate something or someone from your life, don't expect others to understand why, and know that you risk others eliminating you. Just keep in mind that you are making your decision according to what is best for you.

Look at this quote:

"The fool tries to do one more thing every day, but the master tries to remove one thing every day." ~ from the text, *Tao Te Ching*

At first, this quote made no sense to me. I kept rereading it repeatedly, but then I got an understanding. I'm not sure if it's what *Tao Te Ching* meant, but here's my interpretation. When you are foolish, you'll try to do things you think will help you in your situation, but the master will remove things that do not serve them.

You may have heard the phrase that less is more. Having just the things that are essential is better than having way too much of unnecessary things. Before you start with eliminating people, do this exercise. Let's begin with a smaller task like cleaning out your closet.

Step 1. Start with getting rid of anything that you have not worn in the past eight months. (This also includes garments you can fit). The special occasion items you may keep.

Step 2. Eliminate shoes you haven't worn in the

past year.

Step 3. Eliminate all accessories–handbags, scarfs, ties, etc.–you have not used within the last six months. Depending on the type of closet you may have, you may also have other items like hats, belts, socks, etc. Eliminate those items if you haven't used them in the last three months.

Step 4. Donate or pass down those items to someone else.

If you followed each step, you may have found it difficult because it's hard to get rid of things, especially if it had sentimental value, but take a step back. You will notice that you can see things clearer, and it will give you a sense of satisfaction.

Because of your bravery, you will be rewarded with a sense of freedom. There's always a reward for letting go of things even when you don't initially feel that there is.

Identify who or what you must eliminate out of your life that causes you not to be the best version of yourself and explain why. Don't limit yourself to one person or thing. If it's many people or things, write them all down.

Choosing to eliminate someone from your life does not mean that you never talk to or see them again. In some cases, you may just limit the number of times you see this person.

Prayer: *Lord, please help me to get rid of anything that is holding me in bondage. Loosen my shackles so that I may be free. Amen.*

Don't sacrifice your happiness for someone else.

What do you need to eliminate & why?

_____

_____

_____

_____

_____

_____

_____

_____

_____

_____

Remember: Others may not understand your decision to remove yourself from certain situations, but it's ok because you are working on yourself.

Notes:

_____

_____

_____

_____

_____

_____

_____

_____

_____

_____

_____

_____

_____

_____

_____

_____

_____

_____

STEP 6: WILLPOWER

Willpower is having the ability to control yourself and being able to say no to things that appeal to you.

We all want what we want when we want it, right? But what happens when what you want is not healthy for you? It causes you more damage than good.

That's when you must decide to make a change, and to accomplish change, you must have willpower!

It's mind over matter! What that means is that you can control a situation or problem by using the mind.

James 4:7

'Submit yourselves therefore to God. Resist the devil, and he will flee from you."

When you give yourself to the Lord, He will give you a sign when you should withstand against something. If you pay close attention to His voice, then you will find it easier to resist the devil and all his no-good tricks. The enemy will realize that he's not fooling you like he used to, and he will leave you alone. However, he won't leave you alone indefinitely because he is faithful to his job, so he will always try to sneak in and weaken you. Therefore, you must continue to submit and resist daily.

For me, I had to resist two things: one, not reliving my painful experiences, and two, retaliation.

For many years, I tried to prove my innocence; it was less about others and more about proving it to myself. Somehow, I blamed myself for the things that happened to me, even though deep down inside I knew I had nothing to do with the predators' behavior. Still, I carried the guilt as though I did. This caused me to relive the individual experiences I had gone through.

I would think of one of my moments and replay it in my mind, trying to identify what I did to deserve such abuse. I would become so consumed with pinpointing where I was at fault. I would go so far back in my thoughts that I could recall vivid details. I could smell the fragrance in the air. I could hear the sounds that were around me. I could see my surroundings. I could even feel what I felt at those times.

I could not continue to go through these cycles because it was destroying me. It interfered with my happiness, with my peace of mind, and it also took a toll on my family.

It took me years to realize the negative effect it had on me. I had to realize that I had to change my way of thinking. Me trying to prove my innocence was doing nothing but bringing me further and further away from a life that I deserved.

I had to pray and ask God to help me with letting that part of me go. It was a struggle because I didn't want to be at fault for any of it, but I also wanted to be free.

I am now aware of those same feelings when they resurface. Those "stinking thoughts" would stand at the door of my mind aggressively knocking before I would open the doors and let them in. I was determined to take control over those thoughts instead of letting them have power over me. At first, the thoughts would knock and linger around, hoping I would give in and open the door because they were used to me peeking through the window blinds.

Little by little, I've gained willpower over my thoughts. They try to come back to visit me from time to time, but the moment they step on my doorstep, I immediately close the blinds, turn up my music, and sing songs to drown out the noise.

The second thing I had to gain willpower over was the spirit of retaliation. I wanted my offenders to hurt as bad as I did. I wanted their dreams to be haunted as much as mine were. I never had the thought of physically killing them, but I wanted them dead. If there was some way to leave their souls empty inside, I thought it would give me the satisfaction that I wanted.

I would envision things like them getting hit by a car and living out the rest of their days crippled and in pain or they would become alcoholics and their habit would cause them to lose everything.

Why? Simple–I was alive, but I was emotionally dead, so it seemed only fair that they should experience what I was experiencing.

Sometimes I would sit and daydream about different scenarios. It would give me an unhealthy high. I can't quite explain the feeling that it gave me without sounding psychotic.

The thing that you give power to rules you, and I did not want those negative thoughts ruling me because it only kept me in bondage.

I had to constantly remind myself of the word of God that says:

Romans 12:19

"Dearly beloved, avenge not yourselves, but rather give place unto wrath: for it is written, Vengeance is mine; I will repay, saith the Lord."

I learned it wasn't up to me to decide if and how they would receive retribution for their wrong. God said, "I see and I know all, so you live and let me worry about handling them."

2 Chronicles 20:15

"…Thus saith the Lord unto you, Be not afraid nor dismayed by reason of this great multitude; for the battle is not yours, but God's."

Things didn't start changing for me until I removed my hand off the situation and let God fight for me because He was much more equipped to deal with my trauma than I was.

Turning my will over to God did not weaken me or erase what I had been through; it strengthened me and gave me power to live.

And when I gained willpower, it didn't bother me nearly as much as it had in the past. I learned that a couple of my offenders had died, and me knowing that gave me no satisfaction because I realized they had a soul just like me. I only pray that they made peace with God before taking their last breath.

"Willpower is like a muscle. The more you train it the stronger it gets." ~ Melissa Garson

"It's not that some people have willpower and some don't. It's that some people are ready to change and others are not."
~James Gordon

Identify something that you must gain power over:

_____

_____

_____

_____

Now ask yourself, *Am I willing to change the narrative?* If your answer is yes, great! Let's start with prayer.

Prayer: *Lord, thank you for giving me a chance to come before you. Right now, I'm pouring out to you the things that I've been allowing to rule over me. I ask that you first give me the strength to let them go and turn them over into your hands. Amen.*

Remember: You are strong, you are brave, and with God's help, **you got this**!

Notes:

_____

_____

_____

_____

_____

_____

_____

_____

_____

_____

_____

_____

_____

_____

_____

_____

_____

_____

_____

_____

_____

_____

STEP 7: COMMITMENT

Making a **commitment** to be healed, free, delivered and so on means that you must dedicate yourself to the cause. A **commitment** obligates you to follow through.

Psalms 37:5

"Commit thy way unto the Lord; trust also in him; and he shall bring it to pass."

Being committed to the process for me was a real struggle at first. I would go back and forth in my head wanting to be free, but most times I felt like it was a mission that was impossible. I experienced hurt at such a young age and continued being abused throughout the years that I almost felt like being free was not in the cards for me.

Even though I desired to be healed, I feared what that would look like for me. I had a few sessions with a couple of Christian therapists who helped me to understand my emotions. One therapist told me I had PTSD and there was hope for me. There were times that I felt as if God was giving me that hope that I needed to heal, but before I could totally heal, something would make me relapse. You'd understand what I mean if you have ever been cut. As time goes by, the cut closes (heals) up, but then you bump the area where you were cut, and you expose the cut all over again.

For me to stop going through that vicious cycle, I had to stay committed to the healing process. That meant that no matter how many times I was being exposed to what caused me to relapse, I had to keep telling myself that I deserved to heal, and I would remind myself of the benefits of being healed, like, not taking my frustration out on my family. I heard these sayings that "hurt people, hurt people" and also "if you never heal from what hurt you, you'll bleed on people who didn't cut you." I didn't want that to be my testimony. Along with encouraging myself, I prayed in my moments of weakness and the Lord gave me the strength to hold on to the progress that I made.

You may find yourself in the same boat as I did, but I can reassure you that no matter what low valleys you may face, you deserve to be healed.

To be successful in your deliverance, you must make a conscious decision to commit to the healing progression you've made. Yes, you may be compelled to stop, but a runner never wins a race by quitting. Anything worth having is worth fighting for and sometimes you will have to fight to remain free of whatever once had you bound. Staying committed to the Lord will help you trust that He will bring you to an expected end. It 's your level of commitment to what you do that will determine your level of success.

As mentioned in step three, you do not want to take short cuts because you will only cheat yourself. Don't sacrifice your happiness for someone else's.

To help you stay committed, write 3 to 5 things that you will accomplish by not giving up. These things will encourage and remind you of the importance of not giving up.

Prayer: *Lord, I ask that you please give me the ability to stay committed to my healing journey. I know that every day may not be easy, and in those times, I ask that you don't allow me to become discouraged or disappointed. Help me hold on tightly to my "why" with both hands. With your help, I know I can make it. Amen.*

Your thoughts:

_____

_____

_____

_____

_____

_____

_____

_____

_____

_____

Remember: You are making a commitment to become a better version of you.

Notes:

_____

_____

_____

_____

_____

_____

_____

_____

_____

_____

_____

_____

_____

_____

_____

_____

_____

_____

STEP 8: EXAMINE

When you **examine** something, you inspect it to discover the details about it, investigating it thoroughly.

Psalms 139:23-24

'Search me, O God, and know my heart: try me, and know my thoughts: And see if there be any wicked way in me, and lead me in the way everlasting."

This step was one of the hardest for me to do because it forced me to take a close look at myself. I had to ask God to search my heart to make sure that I didn't have any bitterness towards any of my abusers, especially the face of seven. There were times that I thought about killing the face of seven. I thought of ways that I could poison him, and it was mainly because he would smile in my face, pretending like everything was peachy. Even though the thoughts were so vivid, I could never bring myself to follow through with any of them because I would always envision how others would feel. He and I outside of God were the only ones to know the whole truth of what happened that God awful night. For him to laugh in my face and enjoy the company of my family was just an insult.

I needed to do some deep soul searching to make sure that I had really forgiven him. I looked at myself daily to make sure I was not feeling any hatred in my heart. I'd wake up and pray, and in my prayer, I'd say, "Lord help me withstand whatever today brings my way with grace." There were days when it seemed like my prayer was not heard, but I would continue to ask God anyway. Now when I think about it, I needed to feel the anguish because once I didn't feel it anymore, I then knew God had finally given me the victory over him.

I often preach that a lot of times we blame everything on the enemy. The enemy did this and the enemy did that, etc. and sometimes it is the "inner me" that caused things to turn out the way they did, and I had to learn the difference. Forgiving Allen, the face of seven, was a major move for me, but I didn't forgive him for him. I forgave him for myself. Being in the state of unforgiveness was giving him way too much power over me, and he didn't deserve to have any power at all.

I participated in a women's prayer event, and my topic was overcoming obstacles. Before I could sit at the table with various women from all walks of life and speak on that topic, I had to be sure that I had forgiven the face of seven, so again I had to do a self-examination. It was time for me to face the music!

One Sunday afternoon, my husband told me that my old church was serving food, so I thought that would be a great opportunity for me to prove myself. We went into the church, and they had the tables setup where all the women were sitting, and the men were upstairs. The men were serving the ladies that evening, so I sat to be served along with everyone else. When the face of seven walked towards the table, I braced myself and looked down so I wouldn't make eye contact. As he walked away, I asked myself, "What was that?" I had to face him head on as if we had no past and he wasn't the source of a ton of my pain.

Again, he came to the table and this time I sat up, straightened my back, and looked him right in his eyes and said hello. I was proud of myself, and I felt good. I sat there with the other ladies, laughing, talking, and eating. When I left the church, I didn't leave angry, hurt, or sad. Though I felt victorious, I wasn't totally convinced that I had forgiven the face of seven. Even though I could address him, I only saw him periodically. I wanted to be a thousand times sure, so I prayed for another opportunity to face him again.

A few weeks went by, and I heard God speak to me and tell me to go to my old church again because they were having an afternoon service, I asked my girls if they wanted to go, and they both said yes. As we drove, it poured down rain.

I said, "Well maybe we should just go to the market first, just in case it gets worse. Plus, we have a lot of time to spare." When I finished shopping, the rain hadn't let up any and we got really wet. I thought the girls were going to say let's just go home, but they didn't (I was secretly hoping they would), so off to church we went. When we arrived at the church, we drove around the corner about three or four times, trying to find a place to park. I considered that to be another sign that it wasn't meant to be. So, what did I do? Sitting at a light, I prayed and said, "Lord if this is your will, let there be a space for me to park." When I drove around the corner again, wouldn't you know it, there was an open space.

As the girls and I headed towards the door, huddled under one umbrella, trying not to get soaked, the heel on my shoe broke. I was so over it, but I was on the steps of the church; there was no turning back at that point. The girls walked in the door, and I limped in, wet and embarrassed. I immediately limped over to a relative of mine and asked if she had another pair of shoes I could wear, and she had a pair of flats in her bag. Thank you, Jesus! I quickly went to her office to get the shoes. While I was changing my shoes, I said a quick prayer that I would gracefully face whatever came my way. With my head held high, back arched and standing short (I'm not tall), I walked out of the office with a confidence that God had my back.

I made it through the entire service without the face of seven having any effect on me; I glorified the Lord as if he was not there at all. After the benediction was over, I made sure not to overlook him. I needed to be sure I faced him because that was the only way I could know if I was healed of the pain that he caused me.

Examination is a process to determine the condition of your heart. If you examine yourself, you can determine what condition your faith is in because you want to make sure that you are in alignment with God and His will. Be patient with yourself because getting to know yourself can take time, but it's rewarding. If you show God how much you want to change for the betterment of yourself, He will help you, but you must come to Him with humility and a heart ready to repent immediately of the shortcomings that He shows you.

2 Corinthians 13:5

"Examine yourselves, whether ye be in the faith; prove your own selves. Know ye not your own selves,

how that Jesus Christ is in you, except ye be
reprobates?"

My childhood celebrity crush, Michael Jackson,
sang "I'm starting with the man in the mirror... if you
want to make the world a better place, take a look at
yourself and make a change!"

Take this time to do a self-examination. Afterwards,
write what you believe you need to work on that is
delaying your healing.

Prayer: *Lord, as I stand before the mirror of self-examination, help me to take a thorough look at myself and see the good, bad, and the ugly. Help me heal from whatever I discover. Help me to deal with each aspect so that I can become a better version of myself. Amen.*

Your thoughts:

_____

_____

_____

_____

_____

Remember: When you examine yourself, you're not doing so to prove you are not worthy of being healed. You are searching your heart to make sure that you move forward with the right intentions.

Notes:

_____

_____

_____

_____

_____

_____

_____

_____

_____

_____

_____

_____

_____

_____

_____

_____

STEP 9: WALK IN YOUR HEALING & WORSHIP

This is the last and most important step of the C.E.W. process.

Walking in your healing is something that you have to own. You must walk with your head up high, knowing that nothing will stop you from moving forward.

Worship will help you along the way. The more you **worship** God, the better you'll feel while taking each step in your new life.

You may second guess your healing by asking yourself, "Am I really over what had me bound for so long? Am I really deserving of such freedom?" It's not uncommon to have those experiences because there's a war in your spirit. The enemy never wants you to be delivered, so he will try to stop your healing and kill your joy because his ultimate goal is to destroy you.

John 8:32

"And ye shall know the truth, and the truth shall make you free."

John 8:36

"If the Son therefore shall make you free, ye shall be free indeed."

God has already given you victory, and now you must come into alignment with your victory through your actions and with your thoughts. You choose to be made free, so now live in that choice, and embrace your healing.

2 Corinthians 5:17

"Therefore if any man be in Christ, he is a new creature: old things are passed away; behold, all things are become new."

I love this scripture because it gives you freedom. Once you submit unto God and walk in His ways, the things that you used to do are no longer relevant.

Psalms 139:14

"I will praise thee; for I am fearfully and wonderfully made: marvellous are thy works; and that my soul knoweth right well."

Romans 12:1

"I beseech you therefore, brethren, by the mercies of God, that ye present your bodies a living sacrifice, holy, acceptable unto God, which is your reasonable service."

A doctor can prescribe medication for your physical body, but only God can prescribe medication for the soul through worship.

"True worship doesn't put on a show or make a fuss; true worship isn't forced, isn't half-hearted, doesn't keep looking at its watch, doesn't worry what the person in the next pew is doing.

True worship is open to God, adoring God, waiting for God, trusting God even in the dark." ~ N. T. Wright

Prayer: *Lord, I ask that you help me claim my deliverance from this day forth. I'm not looking back at what was. Help me to focus on what is to come. Order my footsteps in your word. Amen.*

Write down a time that you can set aside to worship God (the length of time can be five minutes or however long you desire. Just make sure the time is intentional) and then write three things that you want to thank God for delivering/healing you from.

Time: _____

Your thoughts:

_____

_____

_____

_____

_____

_____

Remember: You are delivered every time the enemy tries to get you to revert to your old self. Watch and pray as you stand guard of your body and mind. Resist the enemy and he will flee.

James 4:7

'Submit yourselves therefore to God. Resist the devil, and he will flee from you."

Notes:

_____

_____

_____

_____

_____

_____

_____

_____

_____

_____

_____

_____

CONGRATULATIONS

You've made it through the C.E.W. process. You've taken all the steps to becoming a better you, and I pray you were healed/are healing from the hurt and pain that you've been going through.

Take one day at a time. Breathe when you feel overwhelmed and be patient with yourself because you are making the change for you!

Remember to pay attention to your C.E.W.'s (Cues)

ABOUT THE AUTHOR

Author, Monique S. Bailey (b. 1975), was born in Chester, PA. She is the lead pastor of Transformation Worship Centre and the former owner of Tiny Tots and Toddlers childcare in Bear, Delaware. Monique Bailey is married to her childhood sweetheart, Blaine, and together they have two beautiful daughters.

Get *In My Despair* on Amazon and Barnes & Noble.com!